Countdown

Ten tiny turtles
sitting on a rock.

2

3

Nine naughty nanny goats
chewing up a sock.

5

Eight enormous emus running just for fun.

Seven slippery snakes
sleeping in the sun.

Six shiny seals
swimming in the ocean.

Five frisky foxes causing a commotion.

Four freckled frogs
sitting where it's cool.

Three chatty chimpanzees playing near a pool.

Two toothy tigers moving like a rocket.

One little joey* riding in my pocket.

* A joey is a baby kangaroo.